WOMAN'S WHIMS.

WOMAN'S WHIMS;

OR THE

FEMALE BAROMETER.

TRANSLATED FROM THE FRENCH

OF

X. B. SAINTINE.

Author of "Picciola."

BY

FAYETTE ROBINSON,

AUTHOR OF "THE CARDINAL," ETC

NEW YORK:

BAKER AND SCRIBNER,

145 NASSAU STREET AND 36 PARK ROW.

1850.

C. W. BENEDICT,

Stereotyper and Printer

201 William street.

TO

AMERICAN COQUETTES,

THIS BOOK

IS VERY RESPECTFULLY DEDICATED

BY THE TRANSLATOR.

PREFACE.

For many years past the book market has been flooded with historical novels and sketches, purporting to give a description of social life in Paris and in France, portraying such gross licentiousness, exhibiting such terrible moral obliquity, that the public mind has become disgusted, and persons have learned to look upon a *French* novel as a thing not to be talked of in polite society, and not to put in the hands of chaste and refined women. No one pretends to doubt the capacity and talent of Dumas, of De Kock, of Sue, and of de Balzac, for the very success of the productions of these writers places their power of enchaining attention beyond dispute, yet there are other authors quite as gifted, the names of whom are comparatively unknown. Among them are de Saintine, D'Arlincourt, Marmier, beyond all comparison one of the most gifted travellers of the day, Clemence Robert, and a host beside, the names of whom have scarcely crossed the Atlantic. In the works of these authors are a depth of true sentiment, a profoundity of thought, and often a wealth of instruction sufficient to remove from French literature the burden of the censure we in this country have been too apt to cast on it.

This censure is entirely unjust. It would be as proper to look on the *tapis Francs* described in the "Mysteries of Paris," as fair exhibitions of the morality of France, to look on the *debauché* students, De Kock loved so well to describe, as specimens of the rising generation of France, to look on the Indiana of Madame Dudevant, as a type of French women, as to look on the books which describe them, as competent to enable the reader to form any idea of the untold wealth of that literature which numbers among its great names the dramatist Moliere, the universal sage Voltaire, of whom with more propriety than of Dr. Goldsmith, may be said,

nil tetigit quad non ornavit,

the classical Racine, the two Chenier, a Villiers, a Cousin, and emphatically the poet of the day, the tender and graceful, though probably weak Lamartine.

We are now experiencing in America what Great Britain felt fifteen years ago, the evil of which was so fully appreciated, that one of the most distinguished of her Reviewers thought it a meet subject for public attention and study. A long and elaborate article in the London Quarterly about twelve years since, sets forth the character of the French translations then overrunning England, in the most unequivocal style.

From this Review, there is little doubt but that much of the prejudice against French literature, has been derived, and there is no doubt but that to a degree this prejudice is well founded. It may not be inappropriate to consider the characteristics of the various writers best known to us. There had been a passion for French literature existing for some time in the country, and persons had turned eagerly to the products of the teeming press of that nation, which since the days of Le Sage had annually put forth not volumes but libraries of those most universal of all fictions, "Sketches of Real Life." The novels of

D'Arlincourt, author of the "Braseur-Roi," of Prosper Merimeé, had scarcely been considered worthy of translation, but when Sue wrote his "Mysteries of Paris," unfolding a depth of social depravity and moral obliquity, of which we in this country are luckily ignorant, the prurient fancy of the public was excited, and a search was made on all sides into the arcana of Parisian book-shops for novels rarely or never mentioned by name even to French women. The Wandering Jew followed, and last of all came the Sea Tales of Sue, which were worthy to live, and which only had he written, would have entitled him to a high place in the list of the great novelists of the day.

The success of these translations excited a yet farther search, and the books of other and minor men were examined into. De Balzac became a hero. "The *Memoires du Diable*" were translated, and also, we believe, the *pean de Chagrin*, one of the most piquant, yet foulest tales of *diablerie* in the language. Without the refinement of the Mephistophiles of German and English Romance, it is yet gracefully enough written to lead astray the untutored mind, and by its gorgeous descriptions of vice, calculated to do ineffable harm. Public taste was now growing decidedly worse, "worse even than that of France," so that not only were the fictions of Paul de Kock really translated, but publishing houses were found base enough to lend their imprint to cover up forgeries which no virtuous woman would confess to any educated man that she had ever read. The public taste at last became cloyed. French depravity and American imitation could produce nothing sufficiently "agacissant," and the world turned from books which were become fade and stupid, to the accounts of the wild revels described in *Le Mauvais Suget*, *André le Savoyard*, *La Laitiere*, etc. The public mind became disgusted with these works, and Dumas appeared on the stage. The "Memoirs of a Physician," the "Three Guardsmen," and the infinity of its continuations, not yet completed, are now occupying public attention, and it is not too much to say, are at least in America, more extensively read than ever were the most admirable of the romances of Sir Walter Scott, the exquisite fictions of La Motte-Fouque, or Goethe's Wilhelm Meister. That they are interesting is undeniable, but so also were Lazarillo de Tormes, and the other Spanish *Picaresque* tales, and the fictions of the writers of the later Greek empire. Dramatised, burlesqued, abridged, and expanded, they have been frequently printed, and people read them with delight and apparent sympathy, though recording nothing more than the intrigues of a corrupt court, and the perils of bands of adventurers, the most meritorious act of each of whom, at the present day, would certainly be consigned to the care of a jailor or hangman.

Madame Dudevant, a writer certainly of immense power, had all the time attracted no little attention. Her history and the character of her writings demand the most careful consideration. A woman, a native of Paris, an *habituée* of the *grand monde*, she was most competent to unfold the evils of the present state of society. Aware, however, of its faults, she seemed to revel in exposing its conventualities, and laid before the public a ghastly picture of the hollowness of the French social system. Had she merely done this; had she not merely displayed the faults, but have told why the faults existed, and have pointed out a means of correcting those errors, the world would have confessed its obligations, and have thanked Madame

Dudevant for her labors, as it is prodigal of thanks to the surgeon, who, with the scalpel lays bare a chronic ulcer that he may bring back health to the system. Madame Dudevant did not do this. She seemed to luxuriate in the portraiture of the depravity of society, and taxed the utmost of her ingenuity to find palliatives and excuses to show that the evils she described were necessities, and that the social system itself was the originator of all the troubles of which men complained. Her books were popular. The innate depravity of Indiana, Stenio, the Countess of Rudolstadt, and her other heroes and heroines, found countless admirers, as people are fascinated by the crimes of great culprits, and read of the atrocity of a Nero, and "*Pedro el crudel.*" Some compensation, however, was due to humanity. Madame Dudevant not only shrank from affixing her name to her own books, but carefully avoided even making her sex responsible for them, and under the assumed name of George Sand, cast before the public volume after volume, which, in spite of her high talent and perfect control of the most flexible of all European tongues, are now rarely or never spoken of except in those *coteries* where Christianity is a name, and the duty of man to act to his fellows as he would have them act towards him is a mere phrase, without meaning and without effect.

We have gone over a list of modern French authors and have formed the above conclusions. We find in the long list of the "men of the pen" of Paris few worthy of treading, even *haud aquo passu* in the steps of Le Sage, or of occupying a place by the side of the yet older novelists. *Le Grand Cyrus* is a better novel than *Les Trois Mousquetaires*, and *Le Diable Boiteux* is worth a thousand of *Le Pean de Chagrin.*

We must not, however, think that French literature is valueless. Clemence Robert has written on a similar subject a better novel than "Anne of Geierstein," though it be almost unknown in our country, and the "Old Convents of Paris" will live when many works now popular in England and America are forgotten. There are, however, books which have taken universal hold of public attention; which have, almost before they were appreciated in the country of their origin, been immediately translated into many tongues. Among these was "Picciola," which has been published in French, English, Italian, Spanish, German and Danish, and which is as popular in its translations as it is in the original. The touching beauty of this tale, the deep insight into the secrets of the human heart which it unfolded, made it everywhere admired, and gave to Xavier Saintine the position of one who had a thorough knowledge of all that actuated his kind. He who found a heroine in an insignificant flower, and who bound all men to himself by the sympathy we must feel for the prisoner, was not unfitted to write on the subject of the secrets of woman's heart.

I do not think *Les Metamorphoses de Femme* a trivial work. I do not think it calculated to make a light impression, but worthy of serious consideration. I have taken a great fancy to it, and in the words of the old English students, "have done it into English," elegantly as I could, and I am sure faithfully. With these few remarks, I submit the following pages to the public.

FAYETTE ROBINSON.

NEW YORK, *March* 20, 1850.

CONTENTS.

LETTER I.

LETTER II.

LETTER III.

LETTER IV.

LETTER V.

PAGE

LETTER VI.

LETTER VII.

LETTER I.

Edward Laguet, Sub-inspector of Finances of the Third Class, to his friend Cyprien Fournier, late Assistant Naturalist of the Jardin des Plantes.

AUXERRE, *March* 15, 18—.

DEAR CYPRIEN:

I read to myself this passage of your last letter: "It is reported that Mlle. Jenny Bouron is to be married in a short time. In the spring the ceremony will take place at the chateau of Neuville, in Normandie. The happy man is known."

I thank you for thus keeping me informed of all the reports of the great city; none of them are unimportant to a poor Parisian like myself, kept in exile for eight months of the year, by the Minister of Finances. In return for your confidence, I shall be as frank myself, but also be more minute. I trust, too, the news will not be uninteresting, for I shall speak of your best friend, that is to say, of myself.

In the month of June last, early in my first tour of duty as a sub-inspector, after having passed sometime in a certain city of one of our richest provinces, I remembered that a charming old lady and intimate friend of my mother, and who had known me from childhood lived in the neighborhood. Her house was but two leagues distant, and one morning after breakfast I set out to go thither. The weather was fine, but a few large clouds were visible in the South. There was, however, no rain, and safe and sound, I reached the home of my old friend, by whom I was received with almost maternal tenderness. She insisted on keeping possession of me for a week; we could not, however, agree, and after a friendly discussion, on this point, she left me to order the room to be prepared which I was to occupy for but a single night. This was my intention.

Taking advantage of her absence, I hastened to throw myself on a sofa in a little room at the end of the passage, the windows of which overlooked some flower beds and an immense kitchen garden. Scarcely had I done so, when the silence and repose around me excited a nervous irritation for which I could give no explanation. We Parisians need either noise and excitement, or else in certain circumstances solitude and calm; solitude when our head and heart are filled with glory and love; calm and contemplation when our eyes rest on some object which excites our thought, or when the ear drinks in some harmony or voices which tell us that life is not far removed. At the time I thought neither of love or glory. I had long ago abandoned both. Did I not make you such a promise? Was I not busy with my report to the Inspector General? To replace this ever present recollection, what was before me? Squares of cabbages and artichokes. Not a sound broke on my ear; not one animal lowed in the surrounding fields; not a bird warbled; not one peasant song was heard. I arose and left the house, the exterior of which I began to examine. All was still; the blinds were shut, no one was in the garden, not a cloud was in the sky. To avoid the heat of the sun which had become intense, I turned into the alleys of the park which lay on the right side of the house.

All there was still and silent as the house had been. The very undergrowth was motionless, not a leaf of any tree moved. There seemed to be no insects, no grasshoppers. The blades of grass, the branches of the trees stood rigidly as *chevaux de frise.* The vegetation seemed artificial. Twenty times I felt myself tempted to seize the branches which hung above me on both sides, and by shaking them awaken an artificial murmur from the leaves. I was in the midst of one of those dead calms which one can experience only in the country or at the Chartreuse. The ennui which this silence and immobility created, induced me to conceive a sudden resolution. I said to myself, I will not remain here a day, not even an hour. I shall die here. I began to contrive a means to extricate myself from a dilemma into which I had become involved, I know not why. This saving means, however—this indispensable pretext which alone could enable me to pass the gates of the purgatory I foresaw, seemed to evade all my powers of invention, so that I was forced to rely only on my Inspector General and my report, which for the last two days had filled every corner of my brain

If, my dear Cyprien, I go into these minute details to you, it is that I may impress on you that nothing in the predisposition of my mind could assist me in the ensuing catastrophe. While I was yet lost in reflection, my mother's friend appeared before me. She came, she said, to keep me company. This phrase implies in the case of a new arrival, the necessity of a tour of inspection from roof to cellar, from boudoir to barn. I had as yet no means of deliverance, and was, therefore, forced to submit to fate. We visited the park together, the immense garden, the farm and pasturage, for my hostess was both lady of the manor and farmer's wife, a conjunction which annoyed me much, for it was evident that the length of my visit would depend not only on the greatness of her possessions, but also on the extent of her knowledge. I tell you, Cyprien, in spite of my respect and deep regard for the old lady, ennui had taken such complete possession of me that I was nearly unable to restrain myself. While she spoke and explained the peculiarities of her *espaliers*, the fleeces of her sheep and the fattening process to which her oxen were subjected, I made answers from time to time, utterly at hazard, for I was thinking only of an opportunity to escape. No suggestion, however, occurred; I saw no possibility of escape, except by means of my Inspector-General. But could even that functionary assist me? I felt an inspiration. I saw the dawn of light. All at once I find in my pocket a letter which in the haste of my departure I had merely glanced at. This letter informs me of the arrival of my inspector. I must go at once to meet him; I have not a moment to lose. But suppose my hostess ask me for the letter! Well, I shall tell her that I have destroyed it. She can believe anything she pleases, but then I shall be away. I shall be safe, in that case, at all events. Thus thought I to myself. I had begun to return towards the house, and had already a distinct perception of the enfilades of rooms, the long stairways I was to ascend and descend, etc. I did not hesitate, and with a brisk air seized the hand of my old friend just as she was about to enter the house. My dear lady, said I, you see a man who is in a great deal of trouble; I have a secret to tell you.

"Indeed," said she. "A secret. So much the better; I admire confidence; speak out, my friend."

I continued with great resolution. My Inspector General—just then a bell rung loudly—"That is dinner," said she; "give me your arm and postpone your secret until dessert."

During the day I had gotten over a great deal of ground, and of all my inner senses, appetite was the one most wide awake. Dinner was after all rather an interruption, than an aggravation of my complaint, so I learned to submit.

When I entered the dining-room I saw an old man come in a mincing gait towards us, and kiss in the most gracious manner the hand of my hostess. I was introduced to him. He was a friend and neighbor. At least, said I, we shall not be *tète-à-tète.* At this I rejoiced, especially as I have a horror of *tète-à-tètes*: just then I discovered that the table was set for four persons.

I pledge you my word, dear Cyprien, that my old oddities of the imagination are entirely suppressed and radically cured. It has been long since I was willing to go half way to meet a foolish passion; since I was wont to nurse such feelings or to believe that they existed elsewhere than in my own head. I was a poet *once.*

Now I am the most matter-of-fact man in France. I only think of the business of my department, and I look for recreation in my leisure hours, only to the positive and mathematical sciences. Do physics and astronomy incline us to hallucination?

As soon, however, as I saw that a fourth person was expected, I was seized with a kind of inexplicable vertigo. The *ennui*, which troubled, distressed, and impelled me to fly from the house, yielded to an altogether different impression,—to a sentiment of satisfaction which I cannot now well explain otherwise than by presentiments and sympathetic affinities. Not a single word had been said in relation to the person who was expected, and whom I already saw in the fourth seat. She seemed to me a graceful and elegant being, all gauze, *mouseline*, and lace. I fancied I saw the tracery of an alabaster hand on the spotless napkin beside her plate. Imagine then my emotion when I saw the door opened, and a pale and tall girl of the most perfect style of beauty advance. You think I fell in love at the first sight. Not at all. Though beautiful, her air was so ungraceful that a most disagreeable impression was created in my mind. She scarcely looked or deigned to bow to the company who had waited long and patiently for her. With body bent mechanically, and eyes cast down during the whole meal, she seemed not to participate in what took place around her. In vain her grandmother—for such is my old friend—at different times made most significant gestures; all was in vain. Her face, her manner, all betokened some unhappiness greater than ennui,—disdain and ill temper.

The old gentleman did not seem to notice her, attending only to the substantials of the table. Our hostess, as if worried of making all the *frais* of the conversation, became silent. The dinner threatened to become monotonous. I put forth all my activity, and sought to excite my companions. The presence of a pretty woman, if it put the old man to sleep, made me talkative. I chattered away, and amid the multitude of things which I said were some happy *jeux des mots*, which procured me a gracious bow from the old gentleman and a smile from the old lady. The young one, however, only looked at me with a contemptuous air. In fine, I was very much dissatisfied with her.

From a feeling of this sort, to falling over head and ears in love, there is but a single step. Though I did not expect it, I was near a catastrophe, and before I left the room experienced the first attack of a true, powerful and intense passion which now is the source of all my joy, torment and hope.

Dessert was served. At this time the storm which I had foreseen in the morning, began with a violent thunder-burst. The wind began to hiss, and the variously-colored clouds flitted to and fro across the heavens. (Their reason for this, probably, was, that they wished to get home before the rain began.) The trees in the park seemed twisted together, and the horizon was hidden by clouds. The spectacle was magnificent. To enjoy it I rose and went to the window. The rain soon began to descend in bucketsfull, and the freshness of the atmosphere, the perfume of the woods, seemed pleasant to my soul as to my senses. The lightning from time to time, seemed, also, to shiver the clouds, amid which it revealed itself in lakes of gold and islands of sparkling silver.

I gave full vent to my contemplation, forgetful, I confess, of the guests, the company of whom I had somewhat abruptly left. Just then a full voice broke on my ear. "My God," said it, "my God." I turned around and saw her. If, however, I had seen another girl in the room, I should have hesitated to recognize in her glowing face, the pale, disdainful beauty I had seen not long before. Her complexion was become clear and brilliant, her brow was smooth as marble, and seemed unclouded, enlarged and purified. It was entirely clear, and in her glance was that instinctive sentiment, that wonderful perception, exclusively reserved for the most exalted minds, of the passionate and intelligent magnificence of the great spectacles of nature.

Each of us for some time stood motionless and silent, but we understood each other. At last words came, at first in exclamations, as if we spoke to our own souls. Our double soliloquy at last assumed the form of dialogue. Though parsimonious in words, she had an incredible facility in expressing her sensations. The sound of her voice added to the value of her thought; the expression of her face made perfect the impression she had excited. As our hostess had not waited for a second thunder-clap to drive her into a room with closely-shut blinds; as the old gentleman, perfectly regardless of the thunder-cloud, yet remained at the table, busied in researches into the profoundities of a bottle of claret, while the *café* and *liqueurs* were prepared, we had ample time to admire the striking tableaux which flitted before our glance. The storm at length passed, and when our hostess returned, the old gentleman left the table. It was impossible, in consequence of the rain, to leave the house, and we went into the drawing room. The old people played piquet, and I approached the chair of the young girl who was busy with her embroidery. I had exhausted the weather, sky and clouds as texts of conversation; I was forced therefore to have recourse to talk of silk and cotton. The young lady, however, came to my assistance and asked me the news from Paris. Cyprien, she had been to Paris; she was in the habit of passing there a part of every year, especially the winter, in the house of an aunt, a lady very rich and very distinguished, the sole heiress of whom she was. The rest of the time she divided between her father, an old soldier, who lived in a neighboring city, and our hostess, who was devoted to her. All this I learned during the evening, not alone from the young lady, but from our hostess, who, though she played piquet, participated in our conversation. You will fancy, my friend, that all night long I did nothing but dream of the young lady. If so, you are mistaken, for I slept soundly. More than that, I resolved that on the next morning I would excuse myself to our hostess, and leave without saying a word to any one else. I had made up my mind to do so, when I received a message from Mme. Bouron, who rose early, that she wished to see me. She wished me to stay a day longer. She had business with her tenants about a renewal of their leases, and with the drovers to whom she wished to sell cattle. I told you she was not only lady of the manor, but a model farmer. All these people would breakfast with her. (It was the custom of the country.) I must help her to entertain this crowd. Could I refuse her such a service?

The drovers and tenants, accompanied by the notary, appeared at the appointed time. I attempted to precipitate myself headlong into the detail of the part I had assumed. I had, however, resolved rather of what I wished to do, than according to my capacity, and financier. as I am, found on this occasion as on many others, that I had made a great mistake. I could not understand the drovers, and the farmer's *patois* was perfectly unintelligible to me. The young girl came to my assistance, after giving me a glance of distrust and pride, without irony, but not without mirth. She spoke to each of the guests, the majority of whom, to tell the truth, she knew. She spoke of all the mysteries of the law of landlord and tenant, in the jargon which is spoken between Orne and Calvados. She appeared kind, merry, sensible, and evidently a good manager. It is true, too, that for the purpose of astonishing me, she spoke very scientifically: perhaps she also sought to laugh at my suffering her to play my part. That, however, matters not, for I became offended at the ease of manner and grace she exhibited. I had rather she had resumed the stern air she bore on the previous evening. In all this I was wrong. Was it possible for her to be ignorant of a language which since her infancy had been spoken about her? With her passion for the country, could she be ignorant of matters which have a real significance to all who know how to appreciate them ? My old friend, the notaries and the farmers having withdrawn to arrange the preliminaries of the contracts which were to be signed, the young lady said:—"This is about the sum total of our society, excepting M. Jolivet, whom you have already learned to appreciate. To these you must add a hunting party, who come here about the end of September, and who are never seen except in their exit or return to the chateau and at meal times, and our recreations are before you. Luckily, however, we can contrive to create others for ourselves." She glanced, as she spoke, across the flower beds arranged before the windows, and then to the little library which was at one end of the room.

To get rid of the farm-yard odor, brought into the room by our new guests, I took it into my head to read poetry, and my hand went instinctively to the *Meditations Poetiques.* As I read, though I knew the verses by heart, my voice became excited, as if I had been reading them for the first time. She too partook of my emotion, for I saw tears in her eyes. She had taken too much delight in the storm of yesterday not to appreciate the poet. At the most interesting moment, and such a moment is easily found when one reads Lamartine, we were interrupted. Her grandmother called her.

"What a pity!" said she: "we will, however, resume the subject. You will not leave at least until you shall have read all to me." The expression of her manner and the sound of her voice as she uttered these words cannot be described.

From this moment, Cyprien, I loved her. I loved her fondly, but with the fondness of a man who can appreciate. At once a factitious illusion arose between us. I had at our first meeting stood *en garde.* I had not adored her, but had studied her. I had been severe even to injustice: for what was her melancholy and reserve, for which I had so much reproached her, but the same ennui which had so severely attacked myself? It was but the exhaustion of an ardent and tender mind, forced to suffer in solitude. It was the vague desperation of an intelligence forced to supply its own wants or to die. To the heart, isolation is death: to the mind it is degradation. She was, however, no longer alone. A being of her own nature was near her. Did she not already experience the effects? To what other cause could I attribute this sudden gaiety, against which in my foolish blindness I had been about to arm myself. I had then to find a pretext to prolong my stay in a house which twenty-four hours before I had been anxious to hurry from. At this time the old lady entered the room alone, and advancing directly towards us, she took my arm and said, "I have not, my child, forgotten that yesterday you promised me a secret. We are alone. What is the secret? Something to do with your Inspector General, eh?" A cold sweat stood upon my forehead, and I wished the Inspector General in purgatory. I had thought of him only in connexion with my escape, and in spite of myself was about to talk of the report I had to make, and the necessity of my speedy departure, when a sudden inspiration seized me, and without knowing precisely whither I was tending, said, "The Inspector General has given me a leave of absence for some days." "Well," said she. "Well, these few days I wish to pass in your house." "Why, then, did you not tell me so this morning?" "Because without your consent I was unwilling to trespass." "Did I not ask you to remain?" "True you did, but I am without suitable apparel." "Is that all?" said the old lady. "Jacques goes to the city to-day, and will pass by your hotel. He can bring all you wish to-night."

I was transported with joy, and kissed her hand as I had seen M. Jolivet do. Our arrangements were concluded without having recourse to the notary, who just then drove off with his clients, the tenants and the drovers.

The next day—but, dear Cyprien, I will not inflict on you an imitation of "the memoirs from St. Helena;" suffice it to say I remained a whole week. I passed eight days by her side, and I do not assert too much, I think, when I say, we lived for each other. How many lovers at first sight have had equal advantages? My hostess having known me from my childhood, did not look on me as a very formidable personage. Thanks to the abandon of country life, my mistress and I rarely left each other. She went out through one door and I by another, but though we started on different paths, those paths always met. These *rencontres* in appearance fortuitous, were the scenes of all our meditations and mutual emotions. At last we did not even take the trouble to seem to walk alone. The old lady sometimes, but rarely, accompanied us. Jolivet showed himself occasionally. He did so, however, always at dinner time.

Cyprien, you are a pitiless and skeptical railer : I fancy I can see you, an Atheist in love, shrug your shoulders at my bucolics. Does love ever manifest itself otherwise than by these countless *naïvetés* to which it is probable you will give another name? I had rather abbreviate my confidence, but in spite of myself I give full vent to my pen, and become intoxicated with my own recollection and story. Give me now all your attention. I had remarked that in the the morning when the sun was bright and birds were lithe, when the meadows were carpeted as it were with the sweet-pea and heliotrope, sparkling with dew, my mistress put herself, so to say, in unison with these concerts, and with the sparkling scenes which surrounded us. She then was talkative, gay and con fiding. When, however, the night was come and the sky was half veiled with clouds, as we watched the fitful wanderings of the scuds across the moon, all the delicious dreams and tender expressions of her heart arose.

One evening she asked me the name of the principal constellations. I am glad it was in my power to give her the information, but you know for some time I have had a decided passion for astronomical science. I pointed towards the north and showed her the seven stars of David's chariot, the polar star, and Cassiopœa with her five luminous points.

She said, "If it be true each one has a star in heaven, that is mine. It is small and humble compared with the others which shine beside it, yet for that reason I have adopted it." She pointed out to me in the east of the horizon, not far from the hair of Berenice, a star of the third magnitude, then very apparent. "Do you know it?" asked she; "have astronomers deigned it a name?"

When she turned towards me to ask this simple question, I was in a kind of ecstatic stupor. My heart beat as if it would burst, and my eyes became moist with tears. I replied, all the time striving to overcome my emotion, that I knew it. "I know it, for it bears one of my names. It is called the heart of Charles, and my name is Charles Edouard."

"It is very strange," murmured she; and after a

moment of abstraction, as if to give full vent to her ideas, said, "*Charles Edouard.* Is not that the name of the Pretender?" She hoped, perhaps, to involve me in a long disquisition on the history of England. It did not do. The very word Pretender dictated my reply, and prescribed the *route* I was to adopt. I took advantage of it. Was it not strange to see astronomy and history thus come to my aid? Science is always valuable.

The confession, which from a feeling of delicacy I had hitherto repressed, burst from me. Note well the fact, my friend, I made it complete. I told her ten times, at every repetition more passionately, clearly and precisely than before.

She no longer sought to disguise her trouble. She did not seek to leave me, but without a word, without a reproach, stood motionless as I made my declaration. Her breathing, however, was short and oppressed, and at length suffering her head to fall between her hands, she sank on a rustic chair which chanced to stand behind her. As I approached and knelt to hear my doom, she reached out her hand, and said, as she suppressed a sigh, "alas, my friend, how much trouble. perhaps, do we prepare for ourselves."

Could I be mistaken? Did she not consent? Should I think so? Her words clearly articulated, her emotion, her sighs, her tears, all gave me right to rely on her. Heaven itself seemed to hear our vows, and to record them in its glittering constellations. Well, Cyprien, this young girl who has given me her heart forever, is Jenny Bouron. The house in which we met, in which we are, is the chateau of Neuville. You may then give a denial to those who say that Jenny Bouron loves another, and that she has consented to marry that person at Neuville.

Your Friend,

CHARLES EDOUARD.

(Such is the name I have adopted, and which I shall henceforth use.)

P. S. Pardon me, Cyprien, for having been so late in telling you of my own affairs, when you are my confident and Mentor in all my follies. This love, however, I have kept shut up in my heart for her and for myself, as in the holiest of tabernacles. In a revelation even to you, dear friend, I seem to commit a profanation. I love her so dearly, and have such confidence in her. Ah, those who calumniate her are wicked indeed.

Adieu.

C. E.

P. S. I am perfectly at ease about Jenny ; yet I would not be sorry to trace these reports to their originators. As you are in Paris, dear Cyprien, I confide the task to you. If you do not know Mme. de Neuflise, the aunt of Jenny, yon can procure an introduction through Maricourt, our mutual friend. I beseech you, Cyprien, come to my aid. See Jenny, once breathe my name to her, and you will know all. Do not neglect my request. I expect a letter from you with impatience.

C. E.

LETTER II.

Cyprien Fournier, late Assistant Naturalist of the Jardin des Plantes, to Edouard Laguet, Sub-inspector of Finances of the Third Class.

PARIS, *April* 4, 18—.

I CONGRATULATE you, my dear friend, on your good fortune, on your Inspector General with the double climax, on your English calembourg, and especially on your astronomy. Astronomy applied to love, must be an important discovery. Now, first of all, let me take you into my confidence. *Et ego in Arcadiam.* I have been in Normandy. Five years ago I was sent by the museum to that beauteous country to examine a breed of cattle recently introduced into France. When I had come to Argentan, like you I remembered an old acquaintance in the neighborhood. This was a college companion. Like you, I set out on foot, for the place was only about four or five miles distant, and the weather seemed magnificent.

Trusting to perfidious advice, to avoid the heat and the dust, I involved myself in interminable cross-roads, shut in by a luxuriant vegetation, which, from time to time, made my progress difficult. One moment my coat tails were fast; at another my hat was knocked off, and when I stooped to seize it, some Hamadryad among the branches caught me by the hair as if to make an Absalom of me. Occasionally my cigar was knocked ten feet from my mouth. The country was peculiarly well watered, and a little stream kept possession of the middle of the path, forcing me to walk like the Colossus of Rhodes, with both feet, however, in the mud. The sun rarely shone on the nymphs of these ripples. At last, however, I extricated myself from the labyrinth, by no means though till like Theocritus' sheep, I had left fragments of my paletot hanging on the wayside thorns.

Thus equipped and covered with mud, with my hands scratched, my face covered with blood, my hair in disorder, my hat crushed and covered with tobacco, I sought to present myself to my old school-fellow.

He was not at home, but I found as his representative, a young widow, his sister, not particularly handsome, but who received me more graciously than I had ever been in my life. When the brother had returned he made me visit his estate and all its dependences. The sister, seeing me as I went, now and then examine a plant, professed herself devoted to botany, and for the purpose of taking lessons, went with me on all occasions, whether her brother was by or not. On the day after my arrival, I fancied she was a charming woman. I adored her on the third, and within twenty-four hours I had reached the delirium of passion. She also seemed to be pleased with me in spite of the scratches on my face, and the grotesque manner of my presentation. When we separated, each of us had hearts red-hot, and made promises to meet soon again. For the first time in my life I thought of marriage without a shiver. Five years since then have passed away, I must tell you, and I, as I have no doubt she does, look back on this affair as a summer dream.

Am I then, as you say, an Atheist in love? No, indeed. What passion, however, is more likely than love to have its illusions, surprises and mirages?

From my own experience and from that of others, I have been led to infer as a general rule that under certain circumstances, it is impossible to pass a week in the country with a woman, never mind who she is, without falling in love. When we get back to the city each one resumes his habits, and these sudden fancies pass away rapidly as the perfumes of gardens and meadows do.

I do not, dear Edouard—Charles Edouard, if you insist on it—fancy for a moment that your love for Miss Bouron is one of mere phrenetic and fugitive tenderness, of which I have just spoken. You are, I admit, an exception to the general rule. Besides, if your love were fugitive, as others have been, circumstances have not been favorable to your shaking it off as soon as usual. You left the country not to precipitate yourself into the whirl-pool of Paris, but to bury yourself in a petty country town. This love which budded under the groves of Neuville has only increased and become expanded in the silence of your office. It matters not: I believe in it, and I am the more induced to do so because, contrary to your usual wont, you kept it a secret even from me. Was not the shock I so involuntarily gave you necessary to arouse that cry of distrust and triumph which were equal almost to a revelation ?

I must now report my progress in discharge of the secret mission you confided to me. According to orders, April 13, I was introduced by Maricourt to Mme. de Neuflise. I have seen Jenny (I once knew her when she was a child,) at the house of her grandmother. She was charming. Who, however, would have recognized your description ?

You described her as a young girl awfully awkward, becoming excited at a storm, talking with drovers, etc. ; a female farm laborer well calculated to shine in a Norman pastoral. The lady, I remember, was a fairy, a queen, a belle of the ball-room. In fine, she was a Parisian *Lionne.* Maricourt presented me to the ladies at a grande *soirce.* You should have seen your Jenny amid the light of countless lamps. Her toilette was dazzling, and she assisted her aunt in doing the honors with wonderful grace. Her bearing was at once easy and dignified, betokening a union of the young girl and of the mistress of the house. Her dignity was perfectly calm and natural, or else was most perfectly studied. To tell the fact, if I had not remembered my business, dear Edouard,—excuse me, Charles Edouard, and do not suffer my rattling to annoy you,—I should have fallen in love with her myself. Rather from duty than from vanity, Mlle. Bouron went to the piano and played an accompaniment to various reedy and tremulous voices, which belonged to sundry young ladies making their debut in the world. You know I hate the piano, which is a terrible instrument of torture intended to throw ill into the midst of the animation of society, and to cut into pieces the most interesting conversation. The piano has become popular in the world only because of the fitness it possesses to be made a handsome article of furniture. I kept myself, then, as much as possible out of the crowd, good thanks to the faculty I possess of looking inwards, while I regulate my countenance into devout attention to external matters. Two romances had been sung unnoticed by me, when two new voices perfectly in accord put an end to my revery and abstraction.

The music which aroused my attention, was a little

duet sung by a lady hidden from me by a group of listeners, and by a tall, fair-haired young man, who glanced tenderly around as he sang. "Thy eyes and my eyes, thy heart and my heart, and all imaginable cupids and blisses."

Prepare yourself, my friend, for a new shock. When the duet was over and the singer arose amid universal murmurs of applause, who, think you, was she? Jenny! Not to hide the truth from you, I pledge my word her voice had been as clear, as vibrating, as full of emotion as that of the man, who critics say, is *fort bien.*

As your agent, I thought it my duty to come at once to an understanding about the man, who is, I learn, a good fellow, with a comfortable fortune, and devoted almost to madness to the worship of the romantic. His name is Beaupre.

After music we had dancing. Jenny waltzed first with the person who sang with her. The peculiar waltz was that *a deux tems*, the most objectionable of waltzes. The country girl you described, after having sung like a syren, described with perfect ease the most difficult gyrations. Leaning on her partner, with her head languid, and resting to his shoulder, her face half buried in an immense bouquet, one might have fancied that intoxicated with perfume, she suffered herself to be carried away by the whirlpools of harmony.

I thought your case was a bad one. That is the happy man, said I to myself, beyond all doubt. I have nothing to do but to write to my friend, and seal it with black. Take comfort, however, Pylades; a few moments after, Jenny was singing and waltzing with others, and I assert with pleasure, which I know you will partake of, that however often she changed her companion at the piano, and her partner in the waltz, whether they were handsome or ugly, she never changed her languid and enamored manner. This I am told is one of the conditions of the *valse a deux tems*.

Though my trouble was somewhat relieved, I resolved to discharge my duty fully, even if it were necessary to make a heavy sacrifice of self love.

I screwed up my courage; I arranged myself, hitched up my cravat, and asked Jenny to waltz. It is a positive fact. You know how *I* dance; I absolutely risked myself, and dared to do so only that I might speak of you.

By way of commencement, between two figures, I asked if she was not the granddaughter of Madame Bouron. She answered that she was. I here replied, I have the honor of a personal acquaintance with your relative, and recently I have heard much of her through one of my intimate friends who passed much time with her during the last fall. Was not that an adroit method of forcing her to ask your name?

She was not long in doing so. "What is the name of your friend?" Edouard Luguet—you do not remember him—"Yes, indeed, I do. I saw him at Neuville. He is a very pleasant man."

As she spoke I examined her very closely, with the expectation of finding some index of trouble or of sympathy. Some *etourdi*, however, interrupted our colloquy, and made all my learned physiognomical observations valueless. I attempted to revive the same subject, but at each of the intervals of the dance, she had so many orders to give, as *aide de maison* to her aunt, that I could not contrive to do so. When, however, I had led her to her place, she asked me, "If my friend was yet devoted to astronomy."

Ponder well on this, Charles Edouard. Examine it well in all its bearings, dearticulate and dissect it. For my own part, I did not know what to think of it, for no sooner were the words out of her mouth, than light as a gazelle, she hurried to the door to receive a party of late comers. I had nothing more to do then than to establish inquiries in relation to her approaching marriage. The preliminary examination of Maricourt had resulted in nothing; you know how discreet he is. Closely, however, as I pressed him, he uttered not one word but the following: "Strange girl."

I had then to strike a new note. Taking an ice, I spoke about it to one of my neighbors whom I had seen already once or twice at the sideboard.

"Bah!" said he. "She is hard to please, as one of these days she will be rich, and knows it." I immediately wrote on my memoranda, "She is rich, and knows it." I had heard a young lad from college call her cousin. As he belonged to the family, he, perhaps, knew more than any one else; as he was a child, perhaps. his confidence was expansive. As he kept himself in the vestibule, half extended on a divan, just as lads rest on the ground when they have a holiday, I sat by him, and said in an insinuating and paternal manner, "are you not a kinsman of Mlle. Jenny Bouron?"

"Why?" said he, with that exquisite college politeness which distinguishes the lads of the fifth from those of the sixth forms.

"Because if so, when she is married you will be one of her groomsmen."

"Oh, to be sure."

"Think you, she will marry soon?"

"Who knows? Jenny is so queer. Only two days ago she insisted on being a nun."

I noted that fact carefully. When I had done with the cousin, I went to the aunt, Mme. de Neuflise. "Your niece," said I, "is a charming person and must have wooers in crowds."

Now must I not be a sincere friend to venture for your sake on such a stupid phrase? Yet I have not repented that I did so.

"My niece," said Madame, "is young enough to wait."

That was a golden sentence, and I treasured it up for you.

This morning I consulted my notes with the following result:

From the fact that she is rich, I conclude that your love is prosperous. She is rich, and will suit you, who are not rich. Some little obstacles must be overcome, but I know you, and have no apprehensions on your account.

From the fact that she is hard to please, and has a right to be so, I gather a good omen. She did not use this right against you, and, therefore, loves or did love you. Do not, however, let us be blind. There was a report of her speedy marriage, for I heard it. The little tattling sylphs of the drawing room, sometimes begotten of a sigh by two meeting glances, rarely report anything entirely fanciful. I am convinced that there was such a report. Perhaps she herself protested against some match, and from that fact resulted her determination to be a nun.

Besides, she can wait; this phrase of the aunt seemed to me but an echo of the words of the niece She can wait. For whom can she wait? Happy day for yourself. At all events you are vain enough to think so.

Hurry, then, and at as early a day as possible become Inspector General of Finances, that you may be worthy of good fortune. To do so, you have only, and I know all the grades of your hierarchy, to skip over the two steps of inspectors, and then wait for the time when you shall be Inspector General. It will need only fifteen years. That time, though, is an immense difficulty we must try by some means to get over. You are a man of imagination. Take the subject into consideration.

Your devoted agent,

CYPRIEN.

LETTER III.

Edouard to Cyprien.

AVALLON, *April* 19, 18—.

DEAR CYPRIEN:

AFTER the lapse of fifteen days of anxiety and torture, I have been forced to hurry on duty from Auxerre to Toncy, thence to Mailly-Chateau, and finally to Virelay; thy letter, with the post-mark of every office in the department, reached me at Avallon, where I now am. Thy letter, dear friend, is the dove of the ark to me. Yes, thou art right; there is something in the report of this marriage. They wished to force Jenny's inclination, and she resisted. Poor girl; she would have become a nun rather than consent, and thus betray our love. She found strength to act as she has done, I am sure in the recollection of our promises. She thought of the heart of Charles.

Thou canst not conceive how this constancy of hers has touched me. I can now scarcely collect my ideas. Joy alone now troubles me, however, for amid the irony which is a condition of thy style, I see clearly that on this occasion thou approvest my happiness and my taste. Is she not, my dear friend, very beautiful? Thou hast seen her in the eclât of her position; I in all her simplicity. At Neuville there was no company, no entertainment, not even a piano on which she could practice. Did she need them to win me? How I love her, Cyprien; I love her as I have never loved before and never shall again. Do not think, either, that I shall wait fifteen years before I shall ask her of her family. I am promised the post of inspector before long. That is something; I have not yet spent all my uncle's fortune, and I am young and ardent. Yes, my lot is cast. The devil take bachelordom. Before I am a month older I shall declare myself to my good old friend, who will be delighted at an alliance of two persons whom she loves. She will be an intercessor for me to Colonel Bouron, Jenny's father, and to Madame de Neuflise, her aunt. One month! Why should I wait a month? Why not do it to-day?

Misericordia! My hand trembles and my sight grows dim. I have just received a letter from Mme. Bouron, dated Neuville, announcing the speedy marriage of Jenny and M. de Beaupré. The report, then, was well founded. By menace and violence they have all been able to triumph over the inclination of Jenny. The couple are to meet at Neuville, and thither the old fool invites me. She relies on me, on my headlong humor, to break the monotony of country life, and to instil some gaiety into a period of betrothal. She wishes me to play my part with the drovers. Take for granted, Cyprien, that I accept the invitation and will be there.

EDOUARD.

LETTER IV.

Cyprien to Edouard.

PARIS, *April* 23, 18—.

FOR heaven's sake, my friend, commit no folly, and give no cause for scandal. I have seen Jenny again. Permit me to give you some information about her. According to my wont, I delayed visiting Mme. de Neuflise until I was afraid to show myself. I asked Maricourt to accompany me. As he dressed, I asked him again about Mlle. Bouron, whom he seemed to know well.

"Strange girl," muttered he, as he had previously done. You know how close-mouthed Maricourt is, and that it is difficult to make him talk. By means of many manœuvres, I contrived to overcome his discretion, and won from him that last winter, at a ball at Countess Pozzoli's, masked for ladies, but costumé for gentlemen, he played the fool either in a Spanish or Turkish dress, and that while wandering about, utterly ignorant of what to do or say, a rose-colored domino, which had occasionally flitted around him, hung on his arm.

The lady had a small foot, a smaller hand in a delicious glove, and two glittering eyes, seen through the satin of her mask. Maricourt soon had his curiosity excited to the highest point, for she revealed to him circumstances of his history he thought entirely unknown. This rose-colored being, amid its revelations, exhibited wild fits of gaiety, and all the airs of a coquette, so as to awaken old recollections and new sentiments, which, as it were, broiled him between two fires. At a given signal the company passed from the ball to the supper room, where masks were cast aside, and in his fair annoyer he recognized Jenny Bouron.

Until that time he had regarded her as a capricious and fantastic girl. (I quote his own expressions.) People like Maricourt, however, the reasonable and cool, seem predestined to fall in love with half crazy women, and our friend became intensely devoted to her.

For some time he was assiduous to the aunt. The young lady, however, in every day costume, was altogether different from the one he had met in masquerade, and all his cold reason was required to crush this passion in its very bud.

When his story was done, Maricourt again repeated the phrase, "singular girl." We then got into a hackney-coach to visit the ladies, for it was raining in torrents.

Edouard, all that happened to Maricourt on the day of the masquerade, except the falling in love, happened to me. I formally retract all my eulogium of the drawing-room fairy. I do not say that I adopt your conclusions blindly, but I appreciate all you experienced when first you saw her. I do not say that I thought her awkward, (gentlemen in love only can use such expressions in relation to a pretty woman) but I found her cold, rigid, and a perfect piece of ice, as Lovelace called Clarissa.

When we entered, she sat beside her aunt with a tambour frame in her hand. She scarcely deigned to lift her head to speak to us, and sat motionless during our whole visit.

But they are about to sacrifice her; they are about to compel her to contract a marriage repugnant to her inclinations. You will say—"can she smile and give vent to mirth while she is unhappy and suffering."

My dear Pylades, despair has not these coagulated appearances. Besides, if she sighed for you, the name of your best friend, and his presence promising her some assistance, should have had a little influence. This was not so. There is some enigma in the affair. I will attempt to divine it. For God's sake, however, do not be precipitate: like Maricourt, call reason to your aid. Do not go to Neuville, I beg and implore you.

Your friend,

CYPRIEN.

LETTER V.

Cyprien to M. de. Maricourt.

PARIS, *May* 8

I will not dine with you to-day, my friend. I write these words hastily, because a post-chaise awaits me in the court yard. In spite of my advice, Edouard has gone to Neuville, where M. de Beaupré has already arrived. I wish to separate the rivals. Adieu.

CYPRIEN.

LETTER VI.

Cyprien to M. de Maricourt.

NEUVILLE, *May* 11.

MY chaise broke down on the road, ten leagues from Nonant, and I was unable to procure any other vehicle, even a country wagon. The slightest delay might have been the cost of a man's life. Judge then how I suffered during the three mortal hours needed for repairs. *En route* again, as the night came on, the most unhappy fancies took possession of me. I recalled Switzerland and the ravine of Bergelbach. I saw the two champions on the ground. They placed themselves *en garde* without the usual salute. Their swords crossed, and I heard the clash of steel. With his usual skill and fortune, Edouard was disarmed at the first pass. Bravo Beaupré. That will do. No! they began again, and Edouard is wounded in the arm. Enough—enough! Explain and shake hands. No! They cross their swords again and fight more madly than ever. Carried away at last by passion, our poor friend precipitates himself on the blade of his enemy. He falls to the ground with a torrent of blood rushing from his mouth.

Such were the pleasant fancies which accompanied me on the whole route.

When I had come to Nonant, and was waiting for the relays to be put to the chaise, I saw a horseman cross the main street. In spite of the darkness, I recognized de Beaupré. I said to myself, all is over—Edouard is dead. I had so fully identified myself with this idea, that I asked but one favor of heaven, that Edouard might be only dying when I was able to reach him. I prayed that he might yet recognize me and enjoy the consolation of having his hands clasped in death by those of a friend.

As I approached Neuville, I contrived from the summit of the hill to get a view of the house, the aspect of which confirmed my prepossessions. There was about the house a most unpromising calm. The second story saloon was lit up, but behind the curtains nothing was moving. The rest of the building was without light, except one room at the corner of the first story, where lights flitted to and fro, as if around the bed of an invalid. We had to leave the route and enter the avenue, whither, as soon as the chaise was visible, a man came. "Are you the doctor?" said he. "No," said the postillion, "it is I;" and he merrily cracked his whip, "Gabriel de Nonant." "Bah!" said the other, as he suddenly disappeared. As soon as I entered the courtyard, I saw the people of the house, who had hurried to meet me, pause in great astonishment, and say, "No, it is not the doctor," and then, without the slightest reference to me, speak together in a low tone.

A single individual with a lantern in his hand, approached and assisted in taking off my trunk. He was pale as I was; I remembered to have seen him at Mme. de Neuflise's, in Paris, on the evening of the soiree, when he presided over the sideboard. He had accompanied his mistress to Neuville. I attempted to say something about the disaster; as if the croup and *Phthysis Laryngitis* had taken hold of my throat, I was able to murmur only a few feeble hissing words I felt half strangled.

The servant with the lantern said, "And does monsieur already know? Poor young man." Then in a voice of deep emotion, he continued, "Only to-day, I do not know why, he gave me ten francs; he was so kind." Putting together the several facts, that the rival had fled, the expectation of the doctor, the disorder and trouble of the whole household, and the emotion of the man with the lantern, could I entertain any doubt? All my apprehensions were realized; a catastrophe had taken place, of which Edouard was the victim. Could I be wrong? Did I not also see color for such a conclusion even in the unreasonable generosity which astonished the recipient. As the doctor was looked for, the patient was yet alive.

"Show me the way," said I to the servant, in my most croupy voice. With his finger he mutely pointed out the way to the vestibule.

I saw that in a time of such confusion, one should not wait to be announced, and hurrying up the passage way, I came to the door of the saloon. On my left was the stairway which led to the room in which I had seen lights. I rushed up four steps at a time, and at the top of the flight of stairs entered a half open door of the saloon, at the extremity of which I saw a chamber.

The twilight of a sick lamp enabled me to see in the depth of this room a bed with curtains. On a table were vials of various kinds and sizes. I paused with a quivering heart, and put my hand on the curtain which shrouded me from my dear Edouard I feared to lift it lest I should disturb the slumberer.

A faint echo of voices in the interior broke on my ear, coming not from the next room, but from one yet more distant. (This was really the one in which I had seen the lights.) The distance of this room aroused immediately in my mind the idea that all was over. My limbs quivered, and perspiration stood on my brow. Resolved to terminate this cruel uncertainty, I lifted up the curtain. Imagine my surprise; I passed from the very depths of despair, as I saw before me not a man but a woman! a young woman, the rosy color and healthy complexion of whom betokened no dangerous illness.

The sleeping invalid was Jenny.

Terrified at my involuntary boldness, and my unexpected good fortune, I suffered the curtains to fall silently, and hurried into the entry, having less knowledge than I had before of what was passing around me. The result of all my conclusions was, however, that dead or alive, Edouard was in the well-lit chamber where I had previously heard whispering, perhaps the prayers for a person *in articulis mortis*. It struck me, however, as strange that Edouard and Jenny should occupy the same *suite* of rooms. This idea, however, did not disturb me a great deal, and I had not courage enough to venture again into the *camera santa* of the bride. At last I found myself at the door of the drawing room, and entered. I looked in vain for the mistress of the house, but saw no one but men, not one of whom seemed to pay the slightest attention to me. All were in a mournful and meditative humor. One had his foot on the rung of a chair with his elbow on his knee, his chin in his palm, his eyebrows corrugated, and his eyes so fixed that he seemed a statue dressed in a blue coat with brass buttons and a black cravat. From a certain family likeness, I at once took it for granted that I saw the Norman colonel, who was Jenny's father. I bowed to him. He did not return my salute. The other man buried in a deep arm-chair, twirled his snuff box around, and from time to time, tapped on its lid. I bowed to him. He turned his head away to take another pinch of snuff. A third one had in his hand the country journal. His mind, however, was elsewhere, for with an air of deep emotion he kept his eyes fixed on the ceiling.

I bowed to him. He answered me with a sigh. I had made the round of the room without meeting any but bronzed faces, to the owners of none of whom did I dare to say a word, for it seemed as if not one of their compressed lips could open except to utter a sentence of death.

All at once, however, I turned around and found a radiant face in front of me. Who, think you, was it? Our friend Edouard, for the death of whom I had been so distressed. Yes, Charles Edouard Laguet fastened himself most pertinaciously to my neck and said, "Victory!" I became more and more bewildered in this labyrinth of mysteries. Within a few minutes, however, we were walking arm in arm in the park.

"Yes," said he, "victory; she loves me; she loves me still; she has never loved another. Victory! My rival—"

"You killed him—"

"What do you mean? I never dreamed of such a thing. Why should I? No; I did better than that; I forced him to yield the ground to me, and he left to-day—in fact not more than two hours ago."

"Ah, it was he, then, whom I met at Nonant?—a pleasant journey to him!"

"Yet, from this sudden departure, inexplicable to all but us, the disarray of the whole house, and the terror I see on every face are derived—"

"There has, then, been a rupture," asked I?

"Yes, a complete one, after an explanation in which she declared positively that she loved another. That was a necessary consequence. On the day before yesterday, Madame Bouron received the letter informing her of my purposed visit to Neuville I only arrived myself to-day—in fact only a few hours before you. You see at once that Jenny was made aware that I was expected—there can be no doubt about that. The idea that we were soon to meet encouraged her. It was this that made her bold. My dear friend, true love gives us such power—"

"Jenny, then, informed you of this?"

"No. How could she? Directly after the explanation, the man went off as if the devil was after him. Then the principal relations, father, grandmother, aunt, all interfered. There was a regular row between them and Jenny, which resulted in the poor child becoming sick. She had a very violent nervous attack, so that they had to put her to bed."

Edouard then told me of his new hopes which were but a revised and corrected edition of the first. In other respects he seemed reasonable enough. It is his intention not to declare himself as yet to the family. He understands that propriety demands some interval to intervene between a betrothal to Beaupré, and to himself. He wishes to have an understanding on this matter with Jenny, who will not be long ill, as the cause of all has hurried towards Paris with the speed of a drunken ballad singer.

When he had told me all he had to say, and had

both thanked and scolded me for my long journey, Edouard stopped in an open space in the park, and in a solemn tone, pointed out a little star lost in the deep azure of the sky.

"There," said he, "is the 'heart of Charles,' the immortal witness of our love, the avenger she ever saw in the silence of her heart, if she once had an idea of betraying me."

I took off my hat and made a low bow to the star, which was about as civil to me as were the mundane beings I had already previously bowed to.

The above, my dear philosopher, were the events of the day, or rather of the evening. In spite of my fatigue, I however contrived to rise at six o'clock to write to you. Edouard, who slept in the next room, awoke me, singing as he did so, a *bravura* from some new opera. May to-day be happy to him as yesterday was, for in spite, dear Maricourt, of my efforts to believe in his star, I have my suspicions. Adieu, dear Maricourt; I shall be, not long after this letter, in Paris.

CYPRIEN.

Edouard to M. de Maricourt.

May 11.

(*This note was inserted in the last letter.*)

We have both loved the same object, and if your passion was not so deep as mine, it was because time and opportunity were wanting to you to ripen it. To-day, she loves me only. I trust, dear Maricourt, our old friendship will not be the price of my happiness, and that when I present you to my wife, you will receive each of us as a friend.

Yours,

E. L.

LETTER VII.

Cyprien to M. de Maricourt.

HAVRE, *May* 15.

I SHOULD be at Paris, but I am at Havre. Why I am, you will learn from the lamentable tale I have to tell. On the day before yesterday, just after I had written, I went into the saloon with Edouard, who had just slipped a few lines for you in the envelope of my letter. We found in the room a few of the Heteroclite figures I had seen the evening before: they seemed, however, to be less austere than previously. The father of Jenny, the Norman colonel, marched up and down the room, with his shoulders bent and his brows corrugated: but he had unbuttoned his coat and put his hands in his pockets, so that he looked less like a colonel and more like a Norman.

The man with the snuff-box was not satisfied with twisting it between his fingers, but from time to time took a pinch and passed it around to his companions. The man of sighs seemed to console himself with some Rheims *biscuits*, which he soaked in Madeira. He was making an appetite for breakfast. After a close examination, I remembered to have seen him at Madame de Neuflise's in Paris, where he had given me some information about Jenny.

Madame de Neuflise at last appeared, and took a seat at the table, with a very melancholy air, which, however, was rather affected than real. The lady of the house soon came and told us that the invalid was much better, and would be able during the day to leave her room.

At this intelligence every brow became brightened. Edouard lifted up his head so rapidly that, his left hand not participating in the motion, he struck himself severely in the cravat. We soon began to talk of recent events: "in all cases it was the best," "when people do not suit it is best to have an explanation," "wooers were abundant," "another as good as Beaupré would certainly appear." At each of these phrases, *laconic as they were lacedemonian*, our friend smiled, blushed, and with difficulty refrained from returning thanks. At the end of the meal all were happy as possible, Edouard being six feet high, and the ex-groom forgotten.

After breakfast Mme. Bouron took me by the arm, and instead of suffering me to return to the saloon, went in the direction of the kitchen garden. I confess I suspect her much of an intention to make me as a stranger examine her agricultural experiments. Luckily, however, Edouard soon joined us under the pretext of inquiring more particularly after the health of Mme. Bouron. He attempted to inquire more particularly into the nature of the rupture. The good lady did not reply to his question, but tucking up her head pointed to him and addressed him in the most ceremonious manner. "You know the monosyllable *vous* instead of *tu*, is like the little black clouds, which sailors when they see them in the horizon, look on as containing a whole tempest in its compass."

Edouard feigned to be astonished, and cast at me a glance which I interpreted to mean as follows, *viz* :

" She knows all; my position forbids me to press the matter. Come to my aid."

I then spoke, following my file-leader. I was not forced to ask twice, for our hostess having enjoined on us the complete discretion, led us to a seat not far distant, and when we had sat by her, said, " Listen, my friends, to the events which took place yesterday. There is a good deal to be said *pro* and *con.* I had no acquaintance with the Parisian lover, and in fact I have no confidence in articles generally from the city of Paris. I was then a little disposed to play at cross-questions with him, and Jenny, you know, sometimes takes queer fancies into her head. Yesterday we could not get her to say a word. We did not know what to think. This morning, however, as soon as she awoke, she owned everything to me ingenuously."

" Edouard gave me a glance which may be translated by, " What did I say? Was I wrong?"

Madame Bouron continued: " This confession did her good. From that time she has been getting better. I scolded her a little, for you know I must play the grandmother." Then turning towards me, she continued, "But, my dear child, if I were to tell you how this match was broken off. See, here is the cause of all the mischief." She pointed towards Edouard.

"I!" exclaimed he with an air of the greatest mock modesty.

"Yes, you are the chief criminal," replied she turning right about towards him. "Last autumn when you passed a few days with the girl, you put ideas into her head—you put ideas—"

"Not an idea which I am unwilling to avouch," said Edouard with the majesty of a tribune.

"My dear child, I know you are a good boy, and I do not reproach you. There is no great harm in giving a young girl a lesson in astronomy. But the child has a lively imagination, and is whimsical. You taught her that her star was called—Monsieur Charles, I think."

"Yes, the heart of Charles—"

"Yes, that is it—you are the prime cause of all that has happened."

Edouard could no longer refrain from declaring

himself, and his brow began to expand, his eye to kindle, and his gesture to become animated.

"You shall hear all," continued the old lady, without paying the least attention to our enthusiastic friend. "Last winter, at a great many places, she met M. de Beaupré. She danced and romped with him without attaching any importance to the affair. Nay, she even quizzed him for his strange manner, and affectation with which he turned up the white of his eyes. He, however, continued to pay her attentions, and like any well-bred lady, she was not insensible to his devotion, though she seemed not to notice it. Things remained in this state until one day monsieur having called when she was not able to receive him, sent her his card. She glanced over it and read those fascinating words, 'CHARLES de Beaupré.'"

"Yes," said our friend, "his name is Charles. A low echo seemed to murmur Charles near her."

"For my part," said the old lady, "I see no particular beauty in the name. That, however, sufficed to change the ideas of Mademoiselle in relation to the gentleman. She took for granted he must be her predestined husband. Observing him, then, more closely, she saw that his person was not without attraction; that in spite of the manner in which he twisted his eyes, when he sang he had a good appearance, and a correct taste in cravats and trinkets. What shall I say? She thought herself obliged to love him, because of his name. Very trifling things suffice to turn a young girl's ideas from right to left."

Turning to Edouard, she said, "You see what a pretty mess you made of your 'heart of Charles!' You are the prime cause of all this."

The good lady without having the slightest idea what dagger thrusts she was giving in the dark, laughed loud and long.

Edouard had lost the power to stand upright. His knees bent, and pale and powerless he resumed his place on the barrel, which placed horizontally, answered us for a seat. As he did so, however, he cast a basilisk's gaze on the good, inoffensive dowager.

"But if Jenny was in love, why did she wish to be a nun?"

"That is all child's play—pure nonsense. She had been to visit her godmother, who is at Picpus. The quiet of the place, her kind reception, and perhaps the costume of the novices took possession of her sacred music, always made a great impression on her. My daughter, Mme. de Neuflise, who told me that story, is satisfied that the organ had most to do with that whim. The first time she heard a waltz the religious fancy took flight."

"At all events, the mere fancy to quit the world proves that she was not much in love with M. de Beaupré."

Edouard, struck with the justness and force of my remark, looked up, approached us, and said "certainly." He could go no farther than this one word.

"Besides," continued I, "this quick rupture and dismissal, given and received with such facility, shows no very deep love on either side."

"You were not there, dear Cyprien," said the old lady, "besides, you do not know Jenny. I have, however, raised her, for I have had the sole duties both of mother and grandmother to play, yet I can scarcely see the whole affair. She explained to me in detail the causes of this rupture, and yet there is some mystery. Perhaps you, who are a savant, may understand them."

The following is her story, and as I am a savant, I drew the psychological inductions, which, dear Maricourt, I am about to submit to you, a philosopher. Let us, however, proceed in logical order, without mingling together the beginning and the end, a thing entirely unexcusable except in treatise on the relations of eternity, the emblem of which is a serpent biting his tail.

"Resolved to lose none of his advantages, M. de Beaupré made his debut at Neuville in a dazzling cravat, in patent boots, and saffron-colored gloves, with an eye-glass, curls, and the air of a conqueror. On the first day he changed his toilette three times, to the great disgust of the colonel, who never admitted any variety in his costume except the buttoning and unbuttoning of his frock, and of Monsieur Jolivet, who fancied that it was necessary for him on the next day to come to the table with fine silk stockings and gold shoe-buckles, which he had not worn for fifteen years before.

"With the instinct of an *artiste*, Jenny had found

out that this costume in a Paris drawing-room became M. de Beaupré very well, but was entirely out of place in the country. She made him understand her. The young man condescended to dress more plainly, to take off the straps of his pantaloons, to wear gaiter shoes, and condescend even to put on a straw hat. In return Jenny gave him a gracious smile. Perhaps, however, she did not like him as well in his new costume.

"Dressed as he said *en paysan*, he wished to act out his role. Not being able to present Jenny with one of Mme. Prenost's *bouquets*, he undertook to manufacture one himself. He was, however, so ignorant of horticulture, that he gathered up only wild chickory and radish blossoms. The young woman laughed not a little at his expense. He laughed with her, though however he fancied her mirth rather too permanent. They visited together the crops and the farm yard. De Beaupré did not, however, like the smell of either the one or the other, and kept his essence bottle all the time at his nose. The smell even of new-mown hay was unpleasant to him. He took no pleasure in strolls beneath the trees, because he did not like catterpillars, and was unwilling to sit on the grass because he was afraid of grasshoppers.

"He objected to visit the top of the hill to see the sun set, because the evening glare was unpleasant. Jenny began to ask herself what she could possibly do in the summer time with such a husband.

On his part, de Beaupré, who had no fancy for the country, as soon as the arrangements between the relations had been completed, resolved to make his proposal in due form to the young lady. One morning he saw Jenny walking alone not far from the flower beds in front of the saloon. He fancied the hour propitious; but was mistaken. She had passed a bad night under the influence of some distant tempest, the air was electrified, and the barometer was descending. Madame Bouron had remarked, as she told us in two parentheses, that when the barometer fell, the gaiety and good humor of Jenny also did.

Remark this point well, Maricourt. It was to me a perfect revelation. Beaupré, however, resolved to make the tender expression, but was, however, much embarrassed. All singers of songs know it will never do to say to a woman, "I love, I adore you," except with a piano accompaniment.

By way of arousing his invention, as soon as he saw Jenny, he inquired after her health, how she had passed the night, and various other *niaiseries*. As they walked along the flower beds, the young girl saw a handful of violets close to the path, covered with the morning dew. She drew near to the young man to avoid treading on the violets, which were of a new variety. De Beaupré interpreted the movement of Jenny as a natural attraction towards the object she loved. The moment was favorable, but the exordium of his wooing was not yet prepared. He taxed his brain to prepare it, and looked for it in every leaf he could snatch at as he passed.

Already predisposed to ill humor by atmospheric influences, Jenny could not refrain, as she saw him tearing to pieces her choicest flowers, from saying :

"Be silent, sir." This was uttered dryly as possible, and she went to the side of an iris from which de Beaupré had been tearing whole branches, as if to protect it.

Whether because he did not understand what

Jenny had said, or because, having found his exordium, he was unwilling to lose it, de Beaupré followed his theme, spoke of an approaching event, he dreamed all blue and gold, of the boldness of his pretensions and of his hopes, which one word could change into certainty. Walking closely by Jenny's side, he looked into her countenance, and with pleasure saw her troubled blush and bended head. He fancied that the avowal he asked for could not be delayed. Sure of happiness, his speech and gesture became animated; he became expressive, eloquent, and passionate. Suddenly, Jenny turned and said, "You are unbearable."

The reason was that the speaker, as he became excited, trampled under his feet violets and mignonettes. His whole path had been that of destruction. Therefore was it Jenny had spoken.

The lover had expected to hear her say:

> "O, bonheur suprême,
> Je t'aime. Je t'aime
> A toi mes amours,
> Toujours, toujours, toujours!"

By the unexpected apostrophe, however, his vanity

was wounded, and with an air of deep vexation he said, "And is it thus, Madame, you receive the expression of my love ?"

"Monsieur, I speak of my violets—not of your love—"

"Is this the reward of the deepest devotion ?"

"My poor mignonettes—"

"I deserve neither your disdain nor your contempt."

"But, Monsieur, you still trample on my flowers !"

"Ah, devil take them—"

"Monsieur—"

"You are a coquette—yes, a coquette—"

"And you a blunderer."

"Ah, I see that it is best I leave you."

"As you please."

"Adieu, then, Mademoiselle. Remember I shall never see you again—never, never—never !"

Away went the beau from the lady, in spite of the reproaches of the aunt, the interference of the grandmother, and the rage of the father against a person who had so severely affronted his daughter.

You now, dear Maricourt, know the whole story of the rupture, not precisely as the good lady told it, but according to my interpretation, and you know I pride myself on understanding not only the people, but cause and effect, the mystery and the clue.

"A lovers' quarrel—all will be arranged;" thus the old lady concluded, when she left us to visit the patient. Edouard, like all men with a lively imagination and keen judgment, always passes from one extreme into another. The intermediate space he neglects, and has no platform for his feet. One hour previous, no one in the world, he was confident, had so certainly inspired a true, powerful and sincere love. A word or two, however, of Mme. Bouron, had sufficed to precipitate him from the summit of his proud certainty into complete discouragement. As soon, however, as he touched bottom, he rebounded, and at the moment I speak, was mid air in regions he was little used to, regions of doubt.

To doubt was to be half right. This, to Edouard, was an immense progress. He had calmly enough heard the old lady end. As soon, however, as our hostess had left us, he said, "Is it possible that Mlle. Bouron last winter took a fancy to that fool? If she forgot me, should I blame her or myself? Perhaps I was wrong in not keeping up some correspondence! A scruple of propriety in this respect, perhaps, has been carried too far—at all events here is one lover dismissed; the bruised violets and mignonettes were but a pretext; at all events I shall soon have an understanding with her."

Soon after noon Jenny entered the saloon, without a trace of emotion on her face. When he saw her so calm, Edouard resumed his hopes

"All this is but a pretence," said he.

She smiled when she spoke to him, and every doubt he had entertained disappeared, so that he at once returned to the seventh heaven.

They walked in the park, and Edouard gave his arm to Jenny. On his return, he had a marble brow and a quailing step. He went into his room, and I followed him. Casting himself into my arms with more evidences of grief than of indignation, he said, "This woman is a monster of duplicity. She denies even the promise she made me, and with an air so calm, so quiet, with such an appearance of deep commiseration for what she called my folly, that I began to suspect myself. I tried to touch her heart by recalling our walks, our studies, our mutual confidences. She assumed an air of pride and dignity which overpowered me."

"And the '*heart of Charles*,'" I said.

"I remember that circumstance perfectly, but your name is Edouard. M. de Beaupré is named Charles." "What do you think of this, Cyprien?" asked he, folding his arms, and giving his voice a hollow, cavernous tone of which I did not think it susceptible; "Is she not the perfect type of dissimulation and falsehood?"

I sought to speak to him, to soothe his excitement, but he at once interrupted me, saying, "Will you go to Havre with me? We can embark at Caen."

I saw that he sought in this long voyage to seek excitement, and I accepted his invitation, expecting the sea-sickness to come to my aid.

Our preparations were soon made, and since yesterday we have been at the Hotel d' Espagne in Havre, the hostess of which is *charmante*. During the voyage, Edouard, like the Heroes of Homer, sombre and motionless, looked at the expanse of the sea and wept. To-day he has gotten over that, and seems to take some pleasure in seeing the jovial sailors dance at the end of the pier, and has amused himself in picking up many-colored pebbles along the shore. Now, dear Maricourt, I am about to begin the psychological explanations I promised you in relation to Jenny. Three of you have loved her, and each at parting has made a different apostrophe. Beaupré thought her a coquette, Edouard thought her a false and dissimulating woman. You said she was a whimsical and capricious girl. To M. de Beaupré I have to say that she is not a coquette. True coquettes have more decided method and more defined attractions, for coquettry is a science, like tactics, and the person of whom we speak obeys too readily her first impulses, is too devoid of calculation and premeditation to be suspected of art and prudence. In relation to her falsity, the same refutation applies. Let us, therefore, pass to your accusation. In the first place, what is a fantastic and capricious woman?

These terms are, or should be, applied particularly to a woman, the ideas of whom are without consistency, and vary without cause. With such a one, thought has no duration and changes perpetually because the will changes, and because there is no conviction. What she desires most earnestly, she disdains as soon as she possesses it; perhaps as soon as she expects it. Her desire is exhausted in the pursuit, and this succession of appetites and wishes springs almost unobserved from the brain, without any modification from events around her. In this instance, however, everything has an external object. Placed in identically the same situations, in an invariable medium, under the same physical influences, Mlle. Bouron would, beyond doubt, preserve a perfect equality of humor and character. To superficial people, who have met her only in the drawing-rooms of Paris, she appeared a young, elegant, and well-behaved lady, though rather prudish and formal.

Others, who had seen her among her flowers, fancied she was a good and simple girl, for she uniformly feels the influence of the objects around her, even of the apparel she wears. The semi-obscurity of a church and the peals of the organ were sufficient to cast her into a religious excitement. A short time afterwards, however, the would-be nun appeared happy, piquant, and merry as possible, as a philosophic friend of mine to his own cost ascertained. She talks with drovers, sings in the morning with birds, and suffers her tears to fall with the evening dew. Sun, moon, and stars each exert a separate attraction for her. To make her happy or melancholy, she needs but a change in the atmosphere. The approach of a storm makes her blood hurry back to her heart, and when the tempest has burst, and the air becomes purified, the blood resumes its course, the spirit becomes buoyant, as the mercury in the barometer does. Jenny is neither a false or capricious woman. She is something worse than either. She is a female barometer.

Yes; I learned this term from her grandmother, and by it I mean to say that she is essentially subject to external impressions, in as much as her susceptibility is purely physical.

Taking advantage of this discovery, I contrived to form a theory in relation to the influences exerted by weight of the atmosphere and inherent magnetism on thinking beings.

Torpedoes, magnetic eels, the nilian silurus, and *tetroadon* are provided with similar electricity. M.

Robin, a distinguished savant, has discovered a similar power in yet another being. Why should this organ only exist in certain varieties of fish? Why, among ourselves, should not the weaker sex be saturated with a nervous fluid? Why should it not have received this strange privilege from nature? I doubt many things more than this.

I think I may affirm that the principle already defined, has its seat in the spleen, an organ to which as yet anatomists have been able to assign no function. I think I will communicate these observations to M. Faraday, who can only be said to have completed his great work on electricity, when he shall have initiated us into the mysteries of the positive and negative poles of woman. Thanks to Jenny Bouron and myself, the physical sciences are about to make a gigantic stride.

* * * * *

Edouard has returned with the pockets of his paletot stuffed and weighed down by pebbles and shells. He found me writing, and I read to him the last page about the female barometer. He smiled, (that is a good sign,) without, however, appearing struck with the excellence of my theory, which, however, I shall not delay on that account to publish.

"Can the character of women, that is to say, their caprice, (falsehood I leave out of consideration,) be subjected to any analysis or appreciation?" Thus he began, "Here your system will fail. Do they act from reason? No. Do not think, Cyprien, I am about to yield to an unjust pique. I am calm and discriminating. I shall soon be cured—but I maintain Jenny did love me."

"Yes, you," said I, "are her country lover—Beaupré was her town lover. There was a combination of two antagonistic influences; two magnetic powers. All, however, is best as it is, for if, unfortunately for yourself and her, you had married her, my dear friend; if you, a dreamer, uninitiated in the mystery of a *valse a deux tems*, had linked your lot with hers, *what would she have done in the winter with such a husband?*"

I was still speaking, when a strip of red clouds encircled the whole seaward horizon, casting its shadow even on Edouard, as he walked up and down the room. He went mechanically to an old barometer in a gilt case, which was hung up in the room rather as an ornament than as an useful article. He touched it with his finger, and the needle made a brisk reply, by moving rapidly ten degrees towards the stormy point.

"Ah, how cross she must be to-day," murmured he.

This murmur, however, was heard. This murmur was the first cry of an apostle, the first confession of faith—Edouard believed.

What a triumph for my system!

Adieu, dear Maricourt; we shall soon meet. To-morrow we return by railroad to Paris.

FOURTH EDITION.

LOS GRINGOS,

AN INSIDE VIEW OF MEXICO AND CALIFORNIA, WITH WANDERINGS IN PERU, CHILI, AND POLYNESIA. BY LIEUTENANT WISE, U.S.N. *Baker & Scribner.*

"Lieutenant Wise has certainly made the best use of his opportunities, and given us a volume, which, for its fresh, joyous humor, its life-like naturalness, its brilliant glimpses of character and manners, and its power of expressive word-painting, we have not seen the equal of, for a long time, in our critical hunt for readable books. No one who runs his eye over the lively table of contents, can satiate his curiosity without a perusal of the entire volume."—*Tribune.*

"He has given the pleasure that Dickens gives to millions, using carelessly, profusely, and *jolily,* two or three of the rarest qualities of genius. For that power of unexpected parallelism, which brings together, suddenly and laughably, the most distant opposites in grotesque similitude; for the quick analysis of a thought or feeling which supplies material for wit; for the genial and irresistible humor which makes what people familiarize by the phrase 'the merriest fellow in the world,' we hardly know the equal of the author of Los Gringos." —*Home Journal.*

"The work itself is one of the most charmingly natural, fresh, and entertaining we have had the pleasure of dwelling over for years. It consists of a series of adventures in California, Mexico, and the Society and Marquesan groups in the far boundless Pacific, and from the first spread of the noble frigate's canvas which bore our author, to the last page, the interest is sustained to the most pleasurable degree by a contiguity of bright-colored, graphic pictures of life on shipboard, scenery, excursions in hunting, life in the rancho, life in the village, city, and on the delightful plains and savage mountains of the glorious regions through which he wandered."—*Albany Atlas.*

"It is a book not to be easily laid aside; something like a companion who talks rapidly and amusing all the evening, whom you cannot find in your heart to remind of the flight of time."—*N. Y. Com. Adv.*

"The author is a person of sharp observation, and has great powers of lively description. His sketches embrace a great variety of subjects, and are not only written in a most entertaining style, but contain much useful information respecting the countries which he visited, and the strange scenes which it was his fortune to witness."—*Boston Courier.*

"He evinces quick observation, a ready faculty of seizing upon whatever is humorous, striking, or characteristic, and an admirable manner of rehearsing a story, or sketching an incident. The book is eminently readable.—*N. Y. Courier & Inquirer.*

"In the varied scenes and adventures he describes, he is entirely *au fait,* and whether on ship or ashore, 'chasing the wild-deer,' or being chased by the grizzly bear, shooting brigands or dancing fandangos, swimming with the Sandwich Island girls, or 'doctoring' interesting young ladies in fits, he is equally *at home.*"—*Literary World.*

NEW PUBLICATIONS.

I.

ALLSTON'S NEW WORK. LECTURES ON ART, AND POEMS By Washington Allston. Edited by Richard H. Dana, Jr. 1 vol. 12mo.

"These are the records of one of the purest spirits and most exalted geniuses of which this country can boast. The intense love of the beautiful, the purity, grace and gentleness which made him incomparably the finest artist of the age, lend their charm and their power to these productions."—*N. Y. Evangelist.*

"The lovers of American Literature and Art will rejoice in the possession of these matured fruits of the genius which seemed alike skilled in the use of the pen and the pencil."—*Newark Daily Advertiser.*

II

MRS. ELLET'S THIRD VOLUME OF THE WOMEN OF THE REVOLUTION. 1 vol. 12mo.

"It consists of almost entirely new matter, gathered with great diligence and good fortune too, from the most obscure sources, and is presented in an engaging style. We think Mrs. Ellet, has accomplished in these three volumes a very useful work in an able manner.—*N. Y. Evangelist.*

III.

WOMAN'S WHIMS, or the Female Barometer. By the Author of Picciola. 1 vol. 12mo, price 37½ cents. An agreeable and picquant love story. Those who wish to enter into the occult mysteries of female barometry, and to comprehend the critical distinctions between dissimulation, caprice and coquetry, will find in this little volume a fund of choice entertainment.

IV.

THE ELLIOTT FAMILY, or the Wrongs of American Women. 1 vol price 50 cents.

V.

CHEAP EDITION OF SACRED SCENES AND CHARACTERS. By J. T. Headley. 1 vol. 12mo., with 12 illustrations by Darley. Uniform with "Sacred Mountains."

"These sketches are among the best he has written."—*The Presbyterian.*

"No one could have drawn the scenes and characters which this volume depicts, whose soul is not attuned to perceive the historical, descriptive and moral beauties of the Bible."—*Watchman and Reflector.*

VI.

SKETCHES AND RAMBLES, by J. T. Headley. 1 vol. 12mo.

"Mr. H. perceives vividly and describes accurately and powerfully. A more agreeable traveller, since Goldsmith, never told his tale."—*N. Y. Evangelist.*

VII.

MISCELLANIES, by J. T. Headley. Authorized Edition; 1 vol. 12mo. Price $1.

"Written with the peculiar boldness of expression, and often displaying the power of vivid dramatic painting, in which the author has no reason to fear a rival."—*N. Y. Tribune.*

BAKER & SCRIBNER, 145 NASSAU ST. NEW YORK.

LETTER FROM WM. H. PRESCOTT, ESQ.

BOSTON, *Jan'y* 30, 1850.

MESSRS. BAKER AND SCRIBNER—

Gentlemen: I understand you are desirous of having my opinion of Mrs. George's "Annals of the Queens of Spain." I will give it to you briefly.

The subject is one that has been hardly touched in the Castilian, and never treated in the English. We have Lives of the Queens of England and of France—the former, by Miss Strickland, an admirable specimen of female portraiture. The present is the first attempt to apply this kind of composition to Spanish history. Yet the lives of the Spanish queens are as fruitful in incident, and full as important, as those of the English—much more so than those of the French, since the operation of the Salic law has prevented women in France from reigning as independent sovereigns in their own right.

There are some embarrassments arising from the great number of petty states which the narrative embraces, which necessarily leads to some details of little importance. But this is compensated by the greater scope and variety afforded for the display of national character and costume.

The author has not shrunk from encountering the difficulties of her task. She has brought the whole range of the Spanish portion of the Peninsula within her plan. For this she has had rare and authentic materials—some of them, in the form of the old chronicles, rich and glowing; while others are too often of the most dreary and discouraging character. She has mastered their contents, however, with commendable diligence. This was the more easy, as they are in her own Castilian; and as a Spaniard she has also been better able to comprehend and enter into the spirit of the Castilian character and usages of a remote age. With these advantages she possesses one, most rare, of writing English with a correctness and copiousness that would exclude the idea of the work being the production of a foreigner.

The earlier pages of the narrative are necessarily occupied with a comparatively barren portion of Spanish history. But as we descend the stream, broader views open on us. The details become more varied and picturesque, checkered with incidents of a tragic character, that give a gloomy interest to the story. The author, in short, having carried her researches into a field hitherto unexplored by the English writers, and not to a great extent by the Spaniards themselves, must be allowed to have made an addition to the sum of our historical lore in regard to the Peninsula. I heartily hope that the book will find favor, and that the enterprise of the publishers will be rewarded by the liberal patronage of the public.

I remain, gentlemen, your obedient serv't,

WM. H. PRESCOTT.

JUVENILE AND MISCELLANEOUS.

CHARLOTTE ELIZABETH'S WORKS, Uniform Edition, 12 vols. 18mo....$6.00
——— in sheep for Libraries and District Schools.................. 7.00

THE PEEP OF DAY, or a series of the earliest religious instruction the infant mind is capable of receiving, with verses illustrative of the subjects. 1 vol. 18mo. with engravings...................... 50

LINE UPON LINE, by the author of "Peep of Day," a second series, 50

PRECEPT UPON PRECEPT, by the author of "Peep of Day," etc. 3d series...................... 50

HERE A LITTLE AND THERE A LITTLE: or Scripture Facts, 4th series. Illustrated (just published)...................... 50

FAIRY TALES AND LEGENDS OF MANY NATIONS, selected and newly told, by C. B. Burkhardt, with original designs and illustrations. 1 vol. 12mo........... 1.13
——— colored plates............ 1.37

ARTHUR'S POPULAR TALES.

KEEPING UP APPEARANCES, or a Tale for the Rich and Poor. 1 vol. 18mo...................... 45

RICHES HAVE WINGS—a Tale for the Rich and Poor, 1 vol. 18mo. 45

RISING IN THE WORLD—a Tale for the Rich and Poor, 1 vol. 18mo. 45

MAKING HASTE TO BE RICH, or the Temptation and Fall, 1 vol. 18mo...................... 45

DEBTOR AND CREDITOR, a Tale for the Times, 1 vol. 18mo........ 45

RETIRING FROM BUSINESS, 1 vol. 18mo...................... 45

The above, bound in uniform volumes in Sheep, for Libraries and District Schools, 6 vols.......... 3.00

WREATHS OF FRIENDSHIP—a beautiful Juvenile Gift Book. By T. S. Arthur. Illustrated with 40 engravings, 1 vol. 12mo.......... 1.50

BURDETT'S HOME STORIES.

LILLA HART, a Tale of New York 1 vol. 18mo., cloth............... 50

THE CONVICT'S CHILD, a Tale of New York, 1 vol. 18mo., cloth.... 56

THE GAMBLER—a Policeman's Story—1 vol. 18mo.............. 45

THEOLOGICAL, HISTORICAL, BIOGRAPHICAL, AND MISCELLANEOUS.

THE PURITANS AND THEIR PRINCIPLES, by the Rev. Edwin Hall, Pastor of the First Congregational Church, Norwalk, Conn. 1 vol. 8vo., third edition........... 2.00

THE ANTIQUITIES OF THE CHRISTIAN CHURCH, translated and compiled from the works of Augusti, with numerous additions from Rheinwald, Siegel and others, by the Rev. Lyman Coleman, 1 vol. 8vo......................... 2.50

THE COMPLETE WORKS OF REV. DANIEL A. CLARK, edited by his son, James Henry Clark, M. D., with a biographical sketch, and an estimate of his powers as a preacher, by Rev. George Shepard, A. M., Professor of Sacred Rhetoric, Bangor Theological Seminary, 2 vols. 8vo...................... 4.00

THE POWER OF THE PULPIT, or Plain Thoughts addressed to Christian Ministers and those who hear them, on the influence of a Preached Gospel. By Gardiner Spring, D. D. 1 vol. 12mo., cloth, with a portrait of the Author, third edition......................... 1.25
——— 1 vol. 8vo............... 1.75

THE BETHEL FLAG, by Gardiner Spring, D. D., 1 vol. 12mo., cloth.. 88
——— 1 vol. 8vo............... 1.25

THE COMPLETE WORKS OF JOHN M. MASON, D.D. Edited by Rev. Ebenezer Mason, 4 vols. 8vo., with a portrait.............. 6.50

THE PSALMS, Translated and Explained for English Readers, by Rev. J. Addison Alexander, D.D., 2 vols. 12mo. (Soon to be issued)..

NAPOLEON AND HIS MARSHALS, By J. T. Headley, 2 vols. 12mo., cloth, gilt. Illustrated with 12 portraits, 20th edition............ 2.50

WASHINGTON AND HIS GENERALS, by J. T. Headley, 2 vols. 12mo., cloth, gilt. Illustrated with 16 portraits, 15th edition.......... 2.50

THE SACRED MOUNTAINS, by J. T. Headley, 1 vol. 8vo., embossed cloth, extra gilt. Illustrated with 12 steel engravings, by Burt—with designs by Lossing, 15th edition...$2.50

——— 12mo., cloth, gilt 1.25

LETTERS FROM ITALY, AND ALPS, AND THE RHINE, by J. T. Headley, 1 vol. 12mo. cloth. A New Edition, Revised and Enlarged. With a Portrait of the Author.............................. 1.25

LIFE OF OLIVER CROMWELL, by J. T. Headley. 1 vol. 12mo., cloth, gilt, with Portrait, 4th edition.............................. 1.25

SCENES IN THE ADIRONDACK MOUNTAINS, by J. T. Headley, with original Designs from Gignoux, Ingham, Durand, Hill, &c., 1 vol. 12mo...................... 1.25

THE ORATORS OF FRANCE—Civil, Revolutionary, and Military. By Cormenin. From the 16th Paris edition. Edited by George H. Colton, with an Essay on the Rise and Progress of French Parliamentary Eloquence, by J. T. Headley, 1 vol. 12mo., 400 pages. Illustrated with Portraits, 4th edition......... 1.25

THE CZAR, HIS COURT AND PEOPLE, including a Tour in Norway and Sweden, by John S. Maxwell, 1 vol. 12mo., cloth, 3d edition 1.00

LECTURES ON SHAKSPEARE, by H. N. Hudson, 2 vols. 12mo., cloth, gilt, 3d edition.................... 2.50

A NEW AND POPULAR WORK ON ASTRONOMY, by Prof. O. M. Mitchell, 1 vol. 12mo., cloth. Illustrated, 3d edition.................

IRELAND'S WELCOME TO THE STRANGER; OR AN EXCURSION THROUGH IRELAND, by Mrs. A. Nicholson, 1 vol. 12mo., cloth.............................. 1.00

——— Library style............ 1.00

AN EXPOSITION OF THE LAW OF BAPTISM, as it regards the mode and the subjects, by the Rev. Edwin Hall, Pastor of the Frst Congregational Church, Norwalk, Conn., third edition, revised and enlarged........................ 75

JOHN'S FIRST BOOK: being a new method of Teaching Children to Read (including the Alphabet and Spelling). Founded on Nature and Reason. By J. Russell Webb, 15

THE OWL CREEK LETTERS AND OTHER CORRESPONDENCE, by W———, 1 vol. 12mo., cloth, gilt........................ 75

THE ORATORS OF THE AMERICAN REVOLUTION, 1 vol. 12mo. by Rev. E. L. Magoon. Cloth. Illustrated with Portraits, 3d edition.............................. 1.25

THE LIVING ORATORS IN AMERICA, by E. L. Magoon, 1 vol. 12mo., with Portraits uniform with Orators of American Revolution.. 1.25

THE WOMEN OF THE AMERICAN REVOLUTION, by Mrs. E. F. Ellet, 1 vol. 12mo. Illustrated with Portraits, 4th edition...... 2.25

TEACHING A SCIENCE: THE TEACHER AN ARTIST, by Rev. B. R. Hall, A. M., author of "Something for Everybody," &c., &c., 1 vol. 12mo....................... 1.00

AURIFODINA, or Adventures in the Gold Region, by Cantell A. Bigly, 1 vol. 12mo...................... 38

GREYSLAER—A ROMANCE OF THE MOHAWK, by C. F. Hoffman, 1 vol. 12mo., 4th edition...... 1.25

THE BORDER WARFARE OF NEW YORK, or Annals of Tryon County, by Hon. W. W. Campbell, 1 vol. 12mo., 2d edition 1.00

THE LIFE AND WRITINGS OF DE WITT CLINTON, by Hon. W. W. Campbell, 1 vol. 8vo.........

——— 1 vol. 12mo..............

HOLIDAYS ABROAD; OR EUROPE FROM THE WEST, by Mrs. C. M. Kirkland, 2 vols. 12mo.

RURAL LETTERS, and other Records of Thoughts at Leisure—embracing Letters from under a Bridge, Open Air Musings in the City, "Invalid Ramble in Germany," "Letters from Watering Places," &c., &c., 1 vol. 12mo...... 1.25

THE FAMILY OF BETHANY, by L. Bonnet; with an Introductory Essay, by the Rev. Hugh White, 1 vol. 18mo...................... 38

ROBERT BURNS AS A POET AND AS A MAN, by Samuel Tyler, author of "Baconian Philosophy," 1 vol. 12mo.............. 75

CLEMENT OF ROME, a Legend of the Sixteenth Century, by Mrs. B. F. Joslin, with an introduction by Prof. Tayler Lewis, 1 vol. 18mo.... 63

www.ingramcontent.com/pod-product-compliance
Lightning Source LLC
LaVergne TN
LVHW011120110826
845150LV00008B/2199
9781425507060